W9-BGV-843

THE GREAT ARTISTS
& THEIR WORLD
VAN GOGH

NEW
FOREST
PRESS

Publisher: Melissa Fairley
Editor: Guy Croton
Designer: Carol Davis
Production Controller: Ed Green
Production Manager: Suzy Kelly

ISBN: 978-1-84898-311-3
Library of Congress Control Number: 2010925215
Tracking number: nfp0004

North American edition copyright © TickTock Entertainment Ltd. 2010
First published in North America in 2010 by New Forest Press,
PO Box 784, Mankato, MN 56002
www.newforestpress.com

Printed in the USA
9 8 7 6 5 4 3 2 1

CONTENTS

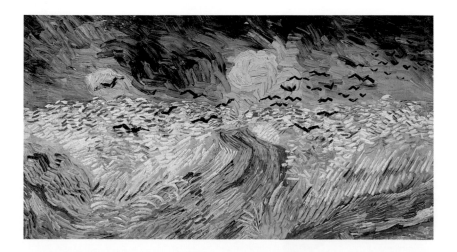

INTRODUCTION

One of the most original and expressive artists ever, Vincent van Gogh is well-known the world over—as much for his tragic life as for his emotional and colorful artwork that has had a powerful and influential impact on art since he died over 120 years ago.

DIFFERENT INFLUENCES

Largely self-taught, Vincent worked as an art dealer, a teacher and an evangelist (a kind of preacher) before becoming an artist. Shunned by many throughout his life, his artwork began selling the day after he died at the age of thirty-seven from shooting himself in a cornfield, and his fame continued to grow. He is now generally considered the greatest Dutch painter after Rembrandt and is extremely important in the development of modern art. His name has been linked to several different art movements including Post-Impressionism, Expressionism, and Symbolism. He was initially influenced by Rembrandt, Rubens, and Gustave Doré, and later by French Realist Jean-François Millet, Japanese prints, the Impressionists, and the Post-Impressionists. Although most people know he was an artist who suffered bouts of madness, there is a great deal more to him. His periods of mental instability were brought on by several illnesses and he never produced art during these attacks. He was also intelligent, thoughtful, and sensitive. In his many letters, written mainly to his younger brother Theo, but also to several others, it can be seen (in his fluent use of three languages) that his love of nature and his view of the world were influenced by a thorough knowledge of art, philosophy, and contemporary literature. Although he did not begin painting until his late twenties and most of his best-known works were created during the final two years of his life, he produced more than 2,000 artworks, including 864 paintings, and 1,200 drawings and prints.

COLOR CHANGE

The eldest of six children, Vincent was the son of a Protestant pastor and grew up in the town of Zundert in the Netherlands. When he was sixteen, he began his first job as an art dealer and traveled between The Hague, London, and Paris. Although keen and industrious at first, he became increasingly odd, rude, or absent and he lost his job. Next, he taught in England, but he had become particularly passionate about his religion, so after a period of studying, he took a job preaching the gospel in a gloomy mining district in south-western Belgium called the Borinage. Unfortunately, he was over-enthusiastic with his preaching and lost his job. While there, he sketched the people around him. Theo, who was now a successful art dealer, encouraged him to become an artist. He studied art in various places,

efore moving to Paris to stay with Theo. In Paris, he met
issarro, Monet, Gauguin, and Signac and, following the
mpressionists' and Post-Impressionists' ideas, lightened his
alette and shortened his brushstrokes. Within two years, he
moved south to Arles in Provence, where the dazzling light
made him brighten his palette even more and develop his
istinctive, expressive style further. With a plan to start an
rtists' colony there, he persuaded Gauguin to join him, but
hey argued violently and after two months, frustrated and
l, Vincent lunged at Gauguin with a razor blade. Gauguin
eft Arles and Vincent sliced off part of his earlobe, nearly
leeding to death. Later, he entered an asylum for treatment.
During that time, he drew and painted, trying out different
methods, marks, compositions, and color combinations.

Eventually, he moved to Auvers-sur-Oise where he was
closer to Theo and where he could be treated by Dr. Gachet,
a modern-thinking physician and amateur artist. He stayed
in Auvers for two months and despite suffering with
frequent depression and other debilitating symptoms,
he worked tirelessly, producing over seventy paintings in
that time that were powerful, dynamic, and colorful. His
swirling brush marks and thick paint in vibrant colors were
unique—and misunderstood. Depression took over and that
July, he shot himself in the chest. Two days later, he died in
Theo's arms of an infection caused by the bullet which had
not been removed. His funeral was attended by many of his
artist friends and supporters and his coffin was covered
with flowers of his favorite colour yellow.

5

THE WORLD IN THE 1880S

It was in the year 1880 that Vincent van Gogh decided to become an artist. The world was changing rapidly, with European imperial powers such as Britain and France continuing to colonize new lands. Africa was being divided. The British defeated the Zulus in 1879 and in 1882 France created a French colony in the Congo which was larger than France itself. In 1877 Britain had proclaimed Queen Victoria "Empress of India," after ruthlessly stamping out a mutiny in its most precious colony some 20 years earlier. Prussia, ruled by Otto von Bismarck, had defeated France and was to build the new republic of Germany. By 1890, half a million immigrants were arriving in the United States of America each year. The modern world was in the making with the invention of the telephone by Alexander Graham Bell in 1876, the first ever phonograph recording by Thomas Edison in 1877, and the invention of the electric light bulb. Alexandre Gustave Eiffel built the *Statue of Liberty* in a Paris suburb before it was shipped to New York in 214 cases in 1884, and then became world famous for his *Eiffel Tower*.

PRIDE OF PARIS

In 1889 the engineer Alexandre Gustave Eiffel built this tower, which stands in the heart of Paris, France, to celebrate the 100th anniversary of the French revolution. It is now famous worldwide as the Eiffel Tower.

COLLAPSE OF EMPIRE

European powers had already colonized many parts of the world and in the 19th century countries such as Britain, Germany, Russia, Italy, and Japan forced China to grant trading rights. This cartoon shows the powers carving up the Chinese cake while the Chinaman looks on in horror.

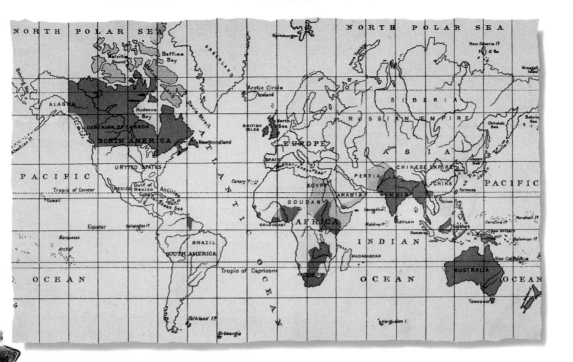

THE ELECTRIC LIGHT BULB

The American Thomas Edison invented the electric light bulb in 1880, making a practical light bulb which glowed brightly as an electric current passed through it. The Englishman Joseph Swan made the same invention independent of Edison in the same year.

BRITANNIA RULES THE WAVES

There were many maps published in the second half of the 19th century which showed British global dominance. The British Empire stretched from Canada to Australia by way of India. Because Britain "ruled the waves" it controlled world trade and was all-powerful. The extent of the empire is shown by those areas colored red on the map. Germany was soon to challenge Britain's supremacy.

THE PACE OF LIFE

The scientific and engineering advances, such as electric lighting, photography, and railway networks, began to change the way in which people lived and worked. The pace of life seemed to be getting faster as the century moved toward its close.

THE WORLD OF VINCENT VAN GOGH

Vincent was the son of a Dutch pastor, Theodorus van Gogh. He was born on March 30, 1853 at Zundert, a village in the south Netherlands. Art was a part of Vincent's upbringing because several uncles in the family were art dealers. Art and religion, therefore, were among Vincent's early experiences as he grew up in the family home alongside his three sisters and two brothers. Vincent tried his hand at many things before turning to painting. He worked in the family art dealing business; turned to religion and preached the gospel, and enrolled at the Academy of Fine Art. In 1880, at the age of 27, Vincent suffered intense depression. He had failed in the family's gallery business, failed as a teacher, failed in love, and had failed in his desire to preach the gospel. Vincent now decided to become an artist. *"In spite of everything I shall rise again…"*

SELF-PORTRAIT WITH A DARK FELT HAT, *(detail)* 1886

At the age of 16, Vincent was apprenticed to The Hague branch of Goupil & Cie, a Paris art publisher specializing in printed graphics. Vincent's godfather, "Uncle Cent," also worked for the firm, as did Vincent's brother Theo. Vincent was to work as an art dealer for seven years during which time he worked both in Paris and London. When lodging in London he fell in love with his landlady's daughter, Eugenie Loyer. Her rejection may have been the reason for Vincent's depression and poor work which finally caused his employer to sack him. Vincent turned to religion.

FARMHOUSES, THE HAGUE, 1883

In October 1880 Vincent decided to enrol at the Academy of Fine Art. He failed to impress his teachers and after his brother Theo agreed to support him financially Vincent moved to The Hague to develop his new career as an artist.

THE PARSONAGE GARDEN AT NUENEN, 1884

Vincent painted obsessively during his years in and around the family home in Nuenen before he finally moved to Paris in 1886. He had little regard for his own well being and would spend his little money on paint rather than food, which resulted in him losing nearly all of his teeth. His brother Theo, who already supported him, said *"...now we must wait and see if he has genius... if he succeeds he will be a great man."*

CLOPPE'S PATISSERIE ON THE CHAMPS ELYSEES

Jean Beraud

The sophistication of Paris was a big change for Vincent. Henri Toulouse-Lautrec and the pointillist painter Paul Signac became good friends with Vincent during his stay in Paris between 1886 and 1888. Every movement of the new revolution in art was spreading out from Paris but, while Vincent tried many styles, he developed his own unique way of painting.

THE ART OF HIS DAY

Even before Vincent had moved to the cosmopolitan world of Paris he was aware of the artistic trends around him. He said in 1885 *"... there is a school I think of Impressionists, but I do not know much about it."* It is certain that in his years working with the art dealers Goupil & Cie in The Hague, Paris, and London Vincent would have been aware of what was happening in the world of art around him, and in the late 19th century Paris was at the very center of that world. When Vincent moved to Paris in 1886 he would have come into contact with many artists through his brother, Theo, who helped sell the paintings of the first real Impressionists, such as Monet, Pissarro, and Sisley. Vincent began experimenting with the *plein air* (open air) way of painting favored by the Impressionists.

THE SALON RUES DES MOULINS, *(detail)* 1894

Henri de Toulouse-Lautrec

Lautrec came from a noble French family. He suffered from a disability which restricted his growth and he sought solace in the sordid nightlife of Paris. His pictures of nightclub scenes are full of movement, color, and life but are also a ruthless portrayal of the seedy side of Paris life.

GARDEN AT VETHEUIL CLAUDE MONET

By the time Vincent came to Paris, Claude Monet was 46 years old and already an artist with a reputation. His painting *Impression, Sunrise* after which the Impressionist movement was named had been painted some 13 years earlier. The influence of the Impressionist painters led Vincent to experiment with color and "plein air" painting.

THE BATHERS *Georges Seurat*

Seurat developed an optical style of painting called *Pointillism*, which used dots of color laid beside one another. When these colored dots were viewed from a distance they blended together "mixing" the colors in the viewer's eye rather than on the canvas. Seurat's fellow pointillist Paul Signac was a good friend of Vincent who borrowed from this style of art in some of his own paintings.

CARNATION, LILY, LILY, ROSE

John Singer Sargent

Sargent was an American artist who trained in Paris but worked in England. Best known for his society portrait pictures, Sargent was aware of Impressionist principles such as "plein air" painting and sometimes adopted them.

GRANDMOTHER READING TO CHILDREN

Mary Cassatt

The two outstanding women Impressionist painters were Berthe Morisot and Mary Cassatt. Cassatt was an American who came to Paris in 1868 in order to paint. Her enthusiasm for Japanese prints was shared by Vincent. She was an accomplished print-maker and produced a set of prints using Japanese techniques. Many of Cassatt's pictures were of domestic scenes because women were not as free as men to paint in the public cafés and boulevards of Paris.

FAMILY & FRIENDS

Vincent relied heavily on his family and friends to support him throughout his life as an artist. It was his brother, Theo, who agreed to support him financially when at the age of 28 Vincent decided to learn how to paint. That support continued until Vincent's death. His love affair with painting was intense and painful, just as his earlier passions for the Church and his unsuccessul relationships with women had been.

PÈRE TANGUY, 1887

Vincent bought his paint from Julien Tanguy's store in Paris. Tanguy, an idealist and former Communard, considered that Vincent and his fellow artists deserved support. Sometimes Vincent exchanged his paintings for supplies of Tanguy's paint. The little back room of Tanguy's store doubled as a gallery and some of the artists we consider to be the founders of 20th-century art, such as van Gogh, Seurat, and Cézanne, exhibited their pictures with Père Tanguy.

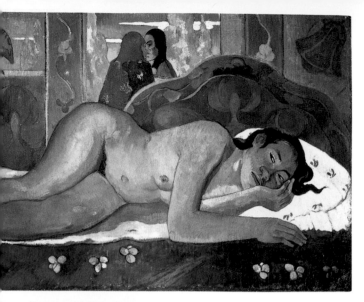

NEVERMORE

Paul Gauguin

Gauguin did not share Vincent's vision of an artist's community dedicated to work (*you must live like a monk who goes to a brothel every other week,* he told another artist friend). Two years after leaving Vincent, Gauguin left France for Tahiti in pursuit of his own dreams. His escape to the South Sea Islands gave him personal freedom from European social conventions and this freedom is reflected in his paintings, which are not bound by the naturalistic conventions of the day.

DOCTOR GACHET, 1890

Paul Gachet was a close friend of Vincent and collected his paintings. His support persuaded Vincent to move to Gachet's home town of Auvers-sur-Oise, near Paris, in May 1890. After the terrible depression and periods of insanity in Arles, Vincent gained a new lease of life in Auvers with the help of Gachet. Not only did Gachet provide friendship but he also convinced Vincent of the value of his work.

VINCENT'S BROTHER, THEO

Vincent's brother was an art dealer in Paris. He regularly sent money from his own income to Vincent to allow him to paint. Theo was devoted to Vincent and christened his own son, born in January 1890, Vincent Willem. Theo was devastated by Vincent's death and survived him by only 6 months, dying on January 25, 1891.

THE LIFE OF VAN GOGH

~MARCH 30, 1852~
A son is stillborn to Theodorus and Anna van Gogh. They name him Vincent

~MARCH 30, 1853~
Another son is born. Theodorus and Anna name him Vincent

~1857~
Vincent's brother, Theo, is born

~1869~
Vincent is apprenticed to the Paris art dealers Goupil & Cie

~1873~
Transferred to London branch of Goupil & Cie. Vincent falls in love with his landlady's daughter, Eugenie Loyer. She rejects him

~1876~
Vincent is sacked from Goupil & Cie. He travels to Ramsgate in England where he gets a job as an assistant teacher. The school moves to London and Vincent takes up preaching at Richmond Methodist Church

~1880~
Moves to Brussels to enrol at the Academy of Fine Art but doesn't stay

~APRIL 1881~
Returns to parents' home in Etten where he falls in love with his cousin Kee Vos. She rejects him

~NOVEMBER 1881~
Moves to The Hague and takes up painting lessons. Falls in love with Sien Hoornik. He lives with Sien and her daughter

The Life of van Gogh

~1883~
Vincent leaves Sien

~1884~
Relationship with Margot Begemann, a neighbor, ends with her attempted suicide

~1885~
Vincent's father dies. Paints *The Potato Eaters*. Moves to Antwerp and enrols in the Academy of Fine Art but teachers reject his work

~1886~
Moves in with Theo in Paris. Theo introduces Vincent to the work of Monet, Renoir, and other Impressionists. Gauguin becomes a good friend

~February 1888~
Moves to Arles in the south of France and dreams of starting an artist's colony

~September 1888~
Seen painting at night, in the town, with candles fixed to his hat

~October 1888~
Gauguin joins Vincent in Arles

~December 23, 1888~
Gauguin decides to leave Arles. Vincent threatens Gauguin with a razor. Gauguin leaves. Vincent cuts off his earlobe with the razor, wraps it in newspaper and gives it to Rachel, a prostitute in a nearby brothel. Theo visits Vincent in hospital

~February 1889~
Vincent taken to hospital suffering from hallucinations. Vincent paints portrait with bandaged ear

FISHING IN THE SPRING, PONT DE CLICHY, 1887

When Vincent moved to Paris in March 1886 his painting style was descriptive. By the time this painting was executed in Spring 1887 he had developed the use of color, his paintings clearly showing the influence of artists such as Monet, Seurat, and Toulouse-Lautrec with whom he mixed. During his stay in Paris he painted over 200 pictures, averaging more than two per week.

TWO CUT SUNFLOWERS, 1887

In the Summer of 1887 Vincent painted his first sunflower pictures. Sunflowers fascinated him; the bright splash of sensuous yellow, the color of sunlight, warmth, and friendship. Sunflowers were to remain a favorite subject for him and he painted them many times. In a letter dated August 1888 when in Arles and anticipating Gauguin's arrival he writes *"Now that I hope to live with Gauguin in a studio of our own, I want to make a decoration for the studio. Nothing but big sunflowers."* Vincent refers to the sunflower as *"...somewhat my own."*

LETTERS HOME

Vincent's letters to his family and friends form a unique record of his life. He wrote regularly to his brother Theo and it is mainly through the existence of this correspondence that we know so much about him today. Vincent stayed with Theo in Paris from March 1886 to February 1888 and of course had no need to send letters to him. As a consequence we know far less about Vincent's life during this period than any other. When he moved to Arles he sent letters every week to Theo and this correspondence describes his struggle with himself and his art.

INTENSE REFLECTION

This self-portrait painted while Vincent lived in Paris shows the influence of the pointillist style. The pointillist painter Paul Signac was a good friend to Vincent during this period. He was exposed to many and varied styles, experimenting with some but ultimately adopting those elements which suited and strengthened the style he was to make his own. Detail of *Self-Portrait, 1886-87, photograph ©1997 The Art Institute of Chicago, All Rights Reserved.*

THE LANGLOIS BRIDGE AT ARLES WITH WOMEN WASHING, 1888

This picture was painted in March 1888, shortly after Vincent moved to Arles. He wrote of the vibrant colors of the Provençal landscape "*...like a Japanese dream...*" His many letters tell of the challenges of painting the landscape, the sea, and the sky, "*...brushstrokes sometimes come thick and fast like words in a conversation or letter...*"

THE FINAL STRUGGLE

"I wish it were all over now..." It is impossible to read the letters written by Vincent toward the end of his life without a deep feeling of sorrow. His illness brought extended periods of madness when he experienced hallucinations complete with voices and visions, but between these attacks he was perfectly well and acutely aware of his condition. In September 1889 he writes *"During the attacks I feel a coward before the pain and suffering... altogether I am now trying to recover like a man who has meant to commit suicide and, finding the water too cold, tries to regain the bank."* This was an indication of what was later to happen. Vincent shot himself on July 27, 1890, dying two days later. His last, unfinished letter to Theo was found on his body and reads *"Well my own work, I am risking my life for it..."* Some think he planned his death in order to increase the value of his work and thereby repay his brother. Vincent had had an arrangement with Theo since 1884 that all paintings he sent to Theo were Theo's property in exchange for the monthly allowance paid to Vincent. Whatever his motive Theo observed *"He has found the peace he never found on earth."*

**THATCHED COTTAGES
BY A HILL, 1890**

Vincent painted this picture in July 1890. He found the village of Auvers *"...very beautiful, among other things a lot of old thatched roofs, which are getting rare."* He was happy in Auvers despite the tragic end to his life.

WHEAT FIELD UNDER CLOUDED SKY, 1890

*"They are infinitely vast wheat fields beneath a dismal sky...
and I have not shied away from the attempt to express sadness and
extreme loneliness... I almost believe these pictures will communicate
to you what I am unable to put into words."*

BROTHERS IN DEATH

Theo arrived on July 28, and sat with Vincent until the end. Vincent's coffin lay in a room hung with all of his last paintings and surrounded by flowers, including, of course, sunflowers. Theo died within months of Vincent and they were buried side by side in the cemetery at Auvers.

THE LIFE OF VAN GOGH

~MAY 1889~
Voluntarily enters mental asylum at St. Rémy

~JULY 1889~
Has another attack while painting outdoors and loses memory as a result of unconsciousness

~SEPTEMBER 3, 1889~
Paintings exhibited at the Salon des Indépendants, Paris

~DECEMBER 1889~
Suffers more attacks and tries to poison himself by swallowing paint

~JANUARY 1890~
Paintings exhibited at Les Vingt, Brussels. The first and only painting to be sold in his lifetime, *The Red Vineyard*, bought for 400 francs

~MARCH 1890~
Ten paintings exhibited at Salon des Indépendants. Monet considers Vincent's paintings to be the best in the show.

~MAY 1890~
Moves to Auvers-sur-Oise to be near Dr. Gachet. Paints 80 paintings

~ JULY 27, 1890~
Goes out for an evening walk and shoots himself in the chest. Returns home to his room at Ravoux's café where Dr. Gachet bandages him and puts him to bed. Spends all the next day in bed smoking his pipe. Theo arrives to comfort him

~ JULY 29, 1890~
Vincent dies on the night of July 29 and is buried the next day

Vincent's "yellow house" was influenced by his enthusiasm for Japanese art. The print on the wall is by Toyokuni and is of Japanese Geishas. Yellow signified the sunshine of the South but also the welcome he always sought. He wrote when traveling South to Arles *"I can still remember vividly how excited I became that winter when traveling from Paris to Arles. How I was constantly on the lookout to see if we had reached Japan yet."*

SELF-PORTRAIT WITH BANDAGED EAR, 1889

One of Vincent's most famous paintings, showing him shortly after he had cut off his earlobe. This was painted in his "yellow house" in Arles.

BLOSSOMING ALMOND TREE, 1890

Painted while in the asylum in St. Rémy in February 1890, only months before his death, Vincent made this simple picture of almond blossom as a present to his brother on the birth of Theo's son, also named Vincent. The picture clearly shows the influence of the Japanese style.

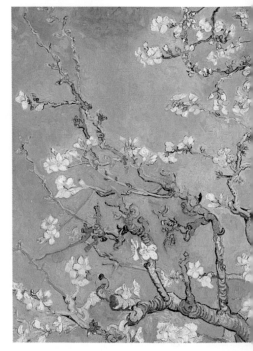

WHAT DO THE PAINTINGS SAY?

Japan's borders had been closed to foreigners for hundreds of years until the 1850s when it was forced to start trading with the outside world. At the Paris World Fair of 1867 Japanese design came to France. At about the same time Japanese prints started to find their way to Europe along with shipped goods. The prints were often used as cheap wrapping paper by the Japanese for whom the prints held no value. Japanese art appeared very exotic to European eyes. The strong colors, decorative design, and flattened perspective became fashionable with European artists, and Vincent was no exception.

PORTRAIT OF AN ACTOR *Toyokuni Go*

Vincent collected a variety of Japanese prints, spending time browsing in a shop which sold prints near his Montmartre flat. His collection eventually grew to around 400 prints.

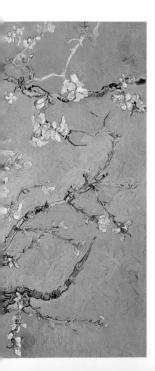

JAPONAISERIE:
FLOWERING
PLUM TREE, 1887

Vincent painted this picture in 1887, while he was living in Paris. The craze for Japanese art affected many but for Vincent it assumed a special importance. He built up a large collection of prints and believed that Japanese art represented a more profound way to depict nature. He began to think that the bright colors and strong light of the South of France would offer a "second Japan" for him.

WHAT DO THE PAINTINGS SAY?

"I am tremendously gripped by the problem of painting night scenes or night-time effects on the spot, actually at night" wrote Vincent. Night scenes appealed to him just as much as the colorful Provence landscape that he had dreamed of and was reality when he moved to Arles in February 1888. In a letter he wrote *"Death may possibly not be the hardest thing in the life of a painter. I must declare I know nothing about them, but when I look at the stars I always start dreaming, as readily as when the black points that indicate towns and villages on a map always start me dreaming. Why, I wonder, should the shining points of the heavens be less accessible to us than the black dots on a map of France? Just as we take a train to reach Tarascon or Rouen, we use death in order to reach a star."*

STARRY NIGHT OVER THE RHONE, 1888

Vincent painted this night scene almost a year before his now world famous *Starry Night*. The intensity of the starlight rivals that of the artificial light shining from the buildings on the riverside.

The couple in the foreground are similar to the couple in *Landscape with Couple Walking and Crescent Moon*. In both cases Vincent appears to have given the man red hair, suggesting that the figure may be himself. In his pictures he has the partner he never found in life.

The figure standing behind the table is described by Vincent as "the landlord." This would be Monsieur Ginoux. His white clothes are painted a lemon yellow reflecting the lighting from the "four lemon-yellow lamps."

THE NIGHT CAFÉ IN THE PLACE LAMARTINE IN ARLES, 1888

When he arrived in Arles, Vincent lodged in the café at the Place Lamartine, his room was over the bar depicted here. His letter to his brother Theo describes the intention behind the painting. Vincent writes *"I have tried to express the terrible passions of humanity by means of red and green. The room is blood red and dark yellow with a green billiard table in the middle."*

A couple sit together, lost in each other and oblivious to the slumped, drunken figures who make up the rest of Ginoux's clientele. The clock above the bar shows a quarter-past midnight.

It is a warm September evening in Arles and a dozen people sit out on the café terrace, the waiter moves amongst them. On the cobbled streets figures stroll under the brilliant starry sky.

THE CAFÉ TERRACE ON THE PLACE DU FORUM, ARLES, AT NIGHT, 1888

The glare of gaslight fills the café canopy with "sulfur yellow and limey green" in this picture painted by Vincent after he had set up his easel in the square at night. He describes *"... a night picture without any black, nothing but beautiful blue and violet and green..."*

WHAT DO THE PAINTINGS SAY?

When Vincent moved to Arles he had hoped to set up an artist's colony. By December 1888 all hope faded as he quarreled with his good friend Gauguin who had come to join him. Alone once again and suffering from fits of depression and actual breakdown, Vincent became a voluntary patient in the asylum at St. Rémy, living in two rooms paid for by his brother Theo. He continued to suffer breakdowns until the end of his life. His pictures are full of emotional intensity as he struggles to paint during periods of calm between the distress of his delusional fits.

The reaper is "the image of death as the great book of nature represents it to us." Vincent's letter of September 1889 to Theo says "...already *I can see myself in the future, when I shall have had some success, regretting my solitude and wretchedness here, when I saw between the iron bars of the cell the reaper in the field below. Misfortune is good for something."*

THE GARDEN OF SAINT PAUL'S HOSPITAL, ST. RÉMY, 1889

Theo paid 800 francs a year for Vincent's stay at the asylum at St. Rémy, near Arles. The building, originally a monastery, was known at the time for its enlightened treatment of the sick. Vincent had two rooms; a bedroom and a studio.

THE REAPER

Vincent was not confined to the asylum and once his confidence returned he went out into the surrounding countryside to paint. At first he painted the nearby fields then a little further out to the hills and cypress trees. *Enclosed Wheat Field with Reaper, 1889.*

WHEAT FIELD WITH CROWS, 1890

In May 1890 Vincent moved to Auvers-sur-Oise, near Paris, to be near Theo. He painted this dark, broody picture of crows struggling in a stormy sky just days before he committed suicide. During the two months at Auvers before his death Vincent painted 70 pictures.

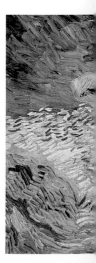

SELF-PORTRAIT, 1889

This picture, painted in September 1889 while at the asylum, is merciless in its self-examination. The eyes, penetrating in their gaze, appear to look deep inside the viewer. Vincent worked during periods of clear thinking and calm between bouts of depression and fits of insanity during which he tried to poison himself by eating his paint.

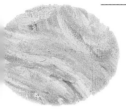

The swirling blue and white lines of the background hint at the sea of instability in which he felt he lived, the chaos of his existence. His bedroom at the asylum had green wallpaper and curtains described by Vincent as "sea-green."

Vincent wrote "*I am in a cage, I am in a cage, and I've got everything I need, fools! I've got everything I could possibly want! Ah dear God, freedom—to be a bird like the other birds.*"

HOW WERE THEY MADE?

*"My dear Theo, Thank you very much for sending
me the canvas and paints which have just arrived...
if on the 10 meters of canvas I paint only
masterpieces half a meter in size and sell them cash
down and at an exorbitant price... nothing will be
easier than to make a fortune on this
consignment."*

It was difficult for Vincent to get
good paints, canvas, and brushes
locally when in the South of France.
Theo sent him supplies to keep up
with his brother's rapid production
of pictures, sometimes several in a day.
By this time, commercially produced artist's
paints were available in tin or lead tubes enabling
artists to transport their materials easily, especially
important for painting outdoors, which Vincent often did.
He would apply paint thickly (impasto), sometimes using a knife
rather than brushes, as the mood would take him. Black lines,
adopted from the Japanese style, can be seen in his paintings.
This helped to set his art apart from the "true" Impressionists
who banished black from their palette.

CANDLE POWER

Vincent is reported to have
attached candles to his easel
and even to the brim of
his hat in order to help
him paint out in the
open at night.

TOOLS OF THE TRADE

Vincent was dependent on Theo
for supplies of artist's materials
which he sent regularly according
to Vincent's needs. In June 1889, Vincent
wrote to Theo from St Rémy;
*"My Dear Theo,
I must beg you again to send me as soon as possible some ordinary
brushes... Half a dozen of each, please; I hope that you are well
and your wife too, and that you are enjoying the fine weather
a little. Here at any rate we have splendid sunshine. As for me,
my health is good, and as for my brain, that will be, let us
hope, a matter of time and patience."*

VASE WITH IRISES AGAINST A YELLOW BACKGROUND, 1890

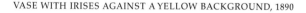

When Vincent was in the asylum at St. Rémy he was free to go into the garden and paint. His studies of lilacs and irises demonstrate that his attraction to the blues and violets of these plants was as compelling as his attraction to the yellows of sunflowers. The deep black outlines filled with vivid blues and use of varnish to highlight the luminous colors make the pictures glow as if they were stained-glass windows. These subjects served to combine Vincent's passion for color with his abiding interest in nature. When Vincent left St. Rémy, the director, Dr. Peyron, said in his final report: "The patient, who was calm on the whole, suffered a number of violent attacks during his stay at the asylum, lasting from a week to a month. During these attacks he was overcome by terrible fears and anxieties, and repeatedly tried to poison himself, either by swallowing paint or by drinking kerosene stolen from the assistants... Between these attacks the patient was absolutely quiet, and devoted himself entirely to his painting."

FAMOUS IMAGES

**VINCENT'S CHAIR
WITH HIS PIPE, 1888**

Vincent painted this picture,
together with one called
Paul Gauguin's Armchair, in
December 1888, shortly before
Gauguin left. Vincent's simple
peasant chair is painted yellow,
the color of sunshine and
warmth, even though it was
made of white wood. This
symbolic coloring of surfaces is
quite typical of his painting.
Vincent's pipe and tobacco are
on the empty chair. In contrast,
on Gauguin's chair rest books
and a candlestick complete with
burning candle. This may allude
to the flame of friendship which
Vincent feared would soon
be extinguished.

Vincent planned to start an artist's community in the South of
France, and when his wealthy art dealer Uncle Cent died and
left Vincent money it was immediately used to refurbish the
rented rooms in the yellow house in Arles. Vincent invited
Gauguin to live with him in the yellow house, and Gauguin
was persuaded not by Vincent but his brother Theo, who
represented Gauguin's work in the Paris galleries. Gauguin agreed
to stay with Vincent as long as Theo gave him a financial allowance.
Gauguin arrived in October 1888 but it seems they did not get on
well despite Vincent's great need for a companion. Gauguin left just
two months later on December 23, 1888.

**VINCENT'S BEDROOM
IN ARLES, 1889**

When Vincent knew Gauguin was
to come to his yellow house he set
about preparing it for his friend.
He painted many pictures which
were hung on the walls of the house
and used to decorate Gauguin's
room. This picture of Vincent's
bedroom is one of two copies he
made in St. Rémy from an original
painted in October 1888 while
Vincent was waiting for his friend to
arrive. Vincent regarded
it as one of his best pictures,
describing it in a letter to Theo
" *In a word, to look at the picture ought
to rest the brain or rather the
imagination.*" The picture has
become one of the most famous
icons in art, its graphic simplicity
underlining the humble way of life
it depicts. In many ways this picture
epitomizes the notion of the
romantic artist who cares for
nothing except his art.

On the table stand two jugs of water, two bottles, two brushes. Either side of the table stand two chairs. Some consider this pairing an anticipation of his friend's arrival, or perhaps something even deeper; his longing for companionship. It echoes his *Starry Night Over the Rhône* and *Landscape with Couple Walking* and *Crescent Moon* where some experts believe Vincent paints himself arm in arm with a companion.

The pictures vary in the different versions, but here they show a self-portrait and a portrait of his sister, Wil. Above the head of the bed hangs a Japanese print.

FAMOUS IMAGES

There was an uneasy relationship between Gauguin and Vincent during the two months in Arles. On December 23, Vincent wrote to Theo saying *"I think myself that Gauguin was a little out of sorts with the good town of Arles, the little yellow house where we work, and especially with me... I think that he will definitely go, or else definitely stay."* Gauguin had in fact already made up his mind to go. Vincent's agitation, caused by the prospect of losing his friend, only served to push Gauguin over the edge and he walked out on the evening of the 23rd. Vincent was unable to cope with this sudden loss, and in a state of emotional turmoil he cut off his earlobe with a razor, wrapped it in a handkerchief then walked to the local brothel where he presented the bizarre gift to a prostitute called Rachel before returning home, where he lapsed into unconsciousness.

Why did Vincent go to the brothel and present a prostitute with his earlobe? Having lost his friend he turned to those who he felt understood him. Artists and prostitutes alike were rejected by society and Vincent felt a kinship with the social outcasts.

Vincent describes the night sky in a letter to Theo *"In the blue depths the stars were sparkling, greenish yellow, white, rose, brighter, flashing more like jewels than they do at home—even in Paris; opals you might call them, emeralds, lapis, rubies, sapphires."*

SELF-PORTRAIT WITH BANDAGED EAR, 1889

The most famous of Vincent's self-portraits shows him back in the yellow house after being treated in hospital following his self-mutilation. Had Rachel not called the police, who found Vincent at home, he would have bled to death. This was the first of many periods of insanity which plagued Vincent until his death.

THE STARRY NIGHT, 1889

The landscape upon which the viewer looks is made from the elements that surrounded Vincent in his asylum; the cluster of olive trees, the little village with its church spire, and the bold dark shape of the cypress tree. However, it is the sky that is overpowering with swirling sea-like lines interspersed with stars exploding like bright fireworks; and the moon, typically painted in Vincent's favorite yellow, glowing in the night sky.

In April 1889 Vincent enters the asylum of St.-Paul-de-Mausole at St. Rémy. Here he is allowed to paint, and to take his paints and easel into the surrounding countryside of olive groves, hills, and tall cypresses black against the bleached landscape of a southern summer. It is perhaps strange but not surprising that what has become the most famous of Vincent's paintings, *The Starry Night*, was painted from memory.

JOSEPH ROULIN, 1889

Roulin and Vincent were the closest of friends. It was Roulin, the local postman, who had helped Vincent home after he had mutilated his ear on that fateful night in December 1888. When Vincent was recuperating in hospital Roulin visited him every day, and Roulin's sons sent reports on Vincent's progress to Theo in Paris because Roulin was unable to write.

LA BERCEUSE (AUGUSTINE ROULIN), 1889

Augustine was the wife of Joseph Roulin and they were neighbors of Vincent in Arles. Vincent painted Joseph, Augustine, and their children. In this painting Augustine can be seen holding a rope, the other end of which was tied to a cradle. By pulling the rope she could rock her baby in its cradle while sitting still for Vincent. As payment for her efforts Vincent allowed her to choose from three portraits he made of her.

THE RED VINEYARD, 1888

Vincent writes in a letter dated November 1888 *"...I'm working now on a vineyard all purple and yellow."* As before, his colors serve to emphasize the overall impression and feeling of the scene. Figures harvest the grapes amid the burning reds of the vines under a merciless sun. In February of the following year Theo writes to tell him that Anne Boch has bought the painting in Brussels for the sum of 400 francs. It now hangs in the Pushkin Museum in Moscow.

THE AUDIENCE FOR THE PICTURES

We know of just one picture sold in Vincent's lifetime, *The Red Vineyard*, painted in 1888, apart from some of his early paintings which were bought by a junk dealer and sold for a few pennies. Those that did not sell were burned. He did however exhibit his paintings, especially toward the end of his life when he was beginning to be known in the galleries in Paris thanks to the efforts of his brother. Three of his paintings were exhibited at the Salon des Artistes Indépendants in Paris in 1888. In 1889 he exhibited pictures in at least two different shows in Brussels as well as the Salon des Indépendants in Paris.

SELF-PORTRAIT

Paul Gauguin

Despite their differences Gauguin was close to Vincent and an admirer of his work. Gauguin kept with him two of Vincent's sunflower paintings, and when he was in Tahiti even ordered sunflower seeds in order that he might cultivate the plants and then paint them. The association with Vincent can never have been far from his mind.

WHAT THE CRITICS SAY

Vincent entered the Academy in Antwerp in 1886 but was at odds with the academic style of tuition, and moved to Paris to be a pupil at the studio of Fernand Cormon, although he stayed only a few months. The Antwerp Academy thought Vincent's work suitable only for the beginners' class. As his work developed so it became more appreciated. Fellow artists such as Toulouse-Lautrec, Signac, Monet, and Gauguin recognized Vincent's work for what it was when they saw it, but initially only his brother Theo and close friends recognized his talent. Gradually, as a few paintings were exhibited here and there, his art received wider recognition. As early as two years after his death a large retrospective exhibition of his work was held, and his fame grew rapidly.

HENRI DE TOULOUSE-LAUTREC

Lautrec studied at the studio of Fernand Cormon and it was through this connection that he knew Vincent. The two became friends and Vincent's painting was to influence Lautrec. It is said that his admiration for Vincent even led Lautrec to challenge to a duel an artist who had spoken ill of Vincent's work.

LES ISOLÉS

— ★ —

NCENT VAN GOGH

out à coup, dés la rentrée dans l'ignoble
x de la rue sale et de la laide vie réelie,
èrent, malgré moi, ces bribes de vers en ma

ranto monotonic
tal, du marbre et de l'eau....
t, méme la couleur noire,
ait fourbi, clair, irisé;
ide enchàssait sa gloire
e rayon cristallisé.....
cataractes pesantes
e des rideaux de cristal
pendaient, éblouissantes,
narailles de métal....

DOCTOR FELIX REY, 1889

Dr. Rey was the doctor who treated Vincent when he arrived at the hospital after he had cut off part of his ear. Dr. Rey was extremely sympathetic and told Theo he would look after Vincent, adding that he was separated from his own brother and understood Theo's worries. Vincent painted this picture of him some weeks later but Dr. Rey was unimpressed and used the picture to block a hole in his chicken shed!

MERCURE DE FRANCE

In January 1890 an article about Vincent's painting by Parisian art critic Albert Aurier appeared in the French newspaper *Mercure de France*. It was full of praise for the artist.

RECOGNITION

Vincent van Gogh is recognized today as one of the greatest painters in the history of European art. The value of his paintings started to increase from the moment of his death. By the 1980s one of the paintings he made of the *The Poet's Garden* (left) was sold in New York for $5.2 million, making it one of the most expensive paintings of all time. This picture was one of several Vincent painted to decorate the walls of Gauguin's room in anticipation of his arrival in Arles. Now when auction houses such as Christie's (right) and Sotheby's sell van Gogh pictures the whole world knows about it.

A LASTING IMPRESSION

The influence of Vincent's art has been far reaching and profound. Vincent wrote *"...instead of trying to reproduce exactly what I see before my eyes, I use color more arbitrarily so as to express myself more forcibly."* His dramatic use of color to convey emotion directly influenced artistic movements such as the Fauvists and the Expressionists, and the effects have rippled through much of 20th-century art.

PORTRAIT OF JOHANNA BONGER

Johanna was Theo's wife. It is thanks to her that we know so much about Vincent's life because she kept all of Vincent's letters to Theo when her husband died. Johanna transcribed the letters which Theo had kept so faithfully and which spanned 18 years of Vincent's life. About 670 letters survive in total. The letters have been reprinted many times in different edited forms since they were first published in 1914.

THE POOL OF LONDON 1906 *André Derain*

Derain was one of the artists who painted in a style called Fauvism. Fauvists, such as Vlaminck and Derain, became aware of Vincent's work when it became more widely exhibited after 1901. Vincent's use of color was taken further by the Fauves who expressed themselves directly through color. Matisse was a famous Fauvist who went on to further develop color and shape to abstraction.

THE MONEY MACHINE

Today Vincent is big business. A wide range of merchandise is created from his pictures all over the world. His paintings can be seen in over 25 major museums and galleries in 10 different countries.

£20 Van Gogh study could

VASE WITH FOURTEEN SUNFLOWERS, 1888

Vincent painted sunflowers again and again during his lifetime. The association between the flower and the artist is now so close that it is not surprising that when one of the sunflower paintings came up for sale in 1989 it fetched the highest price ever paid for a painting at that time. It was sold through Sotheby's to the Yasuda Fire & Marine Insurance Company, Tokyo, and the sale made headlines around the world.

DID YOU KNOW?
FASCINATING FACTS ABOUT THE ARTIST AND THE TIMES IN WHICH HE WORKED

- Exactly one year before Vincent was born, his parents had another child they called Vincent, but this first baby was stillborn. Vincent grew up near the cemetery where this brother was buried. Many historians believe that seeing his own name and almost his own birthdate on a gravestone possibly had a deep psychological impact on him.

- Vincent read many books on art and philosophy and he copied out sentences that he found particularly informative.

- While he lived in Antwerp (from 1885 to 1886), Vincent lost about ten teeth through malnutrition and ill-health, as he spent his allowance on painting materials rather than food.

- In Antwerp, he did not pay his bills, but used the money he saved to buy a train ticket to Paris.

- When he first began painting, Vincent used dark earth colors such as raw umber, raw sienna, and olive green. As new chemical pigments were developed and he saw the work of the Impressionists, he changed his palette to bright colors, including zinc white, raw sienna, yellow ochre, chrome yellow, red alizarin lake, ultramarine, cobalt blue, viridian, emerald green, and chrome green.

- While Vincent was alive, most people did not appreciate that he was not trying to copy reality or to imitate nature, but to express emotion.

- The Impressionists painted light falling on objects, but Vincent painted objects that radiated with their own inner light.

- His understanding of the use of color was transformed by reading the work of the art critic Charles Blanc who described how Delacroix used color.

- In the ten years he worked as an artist, among his huge output, Vincent painted thirty-six self-portraits and wrote over 800 letters to family and friends. His earliest surviving self-portrait was painted in 1886 and the last was painted in 1889.

- He took piano lessons for a short time, but the teacher refused to teach him after he insisted that the piano notes ranged in color from blue to yellow.

- Yellow signified happiness to Vincent. In Dutch literature, sunflowers were a symbol of devotion and loyalty.

- Vincent always felt he had a lot to learn and particularly about painting, so he was keen to listen to Gauguin's advice when he stayed at Arles, but Gauguin's constant criticisms distressed him and badly affected his health.

- During his stay at the St. Remy asylum, Vincent sometimes produced paintings based on prints by some of his favorite artists, including Millet, Delacroix, and Rembrandt.

- His influence on Expressionism, Fauvism, abstraction, and other aspects of twentieth century art was enormous.

- The van Gogh museum in Amsterdam contains the largest collection of his work consisting of more than 200 paintings, 437 drawings, and thirty-one prints.

- Vincent's work now ranks among the most expensive in the world.

- As well as other mental and physical conditions, Vincent suffered from epilepsy and schizophrenia.

- In the painting *Starry Night*, it is believed that Vincent referred to a story in the Old Testament, when Joseph says to his eleven brothers: "I have had another dream. I saw the sun, the moon, and eleven stars bowing to me."

- In the two years he spent in Arles, Vincent produced one hundred landscapes, fifty portraits, forty still lifes, and approximately one hundred drawings.

- Vincent first began collecting Japanese prints in 1885 in Antwerp and continued buying them when he moved to France.

- He signed most of his works Vincent because he believed that van Gogh was too difficult for people to pronounce. Many of his works are not signed at all, because he felt it was arrogant.

- Between 1886 and 1888 his paintings were made up of small dashes, but from 1888 to 1890 he painted in thick waves and swirls.

He followed the color theories that the Impressionists embraced, including placing complementary colors next to each other to make them appear brighter, but he also created his own color theories. For instance, he painted yellow sunflowers against a blue background and again against a paler yellow background. Whatever he did, he made colors appear brighter than ever.

SUMMARY TIMELINE OF
THE ARTIST & HIS CONTEMPORARIES

THE LIFE OF VAN GOGH

~1853~

In the year of van Gogh's birth, the first potato chips are made in America

~1855~

Over five million people visit the first Exhibition Universelle held in Paris; London's first pillar box is placed in Fleet Street

~1856~

The first synthetic organic dye, mauveine, is discovered by accident by William Henry Perkin—triggering a fashion for the color mauve; the artist John Singer Sargent is born

~1857~

In the year that Theo is born, the first world economic crisis begins in New York; earthquakes strike in California, Tokyo, and Naples

~1858~

Ottawa becomes the capital

of Canada; Macy's department store opens in New York City; the can-can is first performed in Paris

~1859~

Naturalist Charles Darwin publishes his controversial book, *On the Origin of Species*

~1861~

Abraham Lincoln becomes President of the United States; the American Civil War begins; Victor Emmanuel II of Sardinia becomes the first king of Italy

~1862~

Otto von Bismarck becomes Prime Minister of Prussia; Gustav Klimt is born; the Red Cross is founded

~1863~

In Paris, the Salon des Refusés displays the work of all the artists who were rejected from the official Salon; Manet's painting *Le Déjeuner sur l'Herbe* shocks the art world; Edvard Munch is born and Delacroix dies

~1864~

Eleven year old Vincent begins drawing for the first time

~1865~

An early version of Tolstoy's *War and Peace* is serialized in a

Russian magazine; the American Civil War ends and slavery is abolished

~1866~

Kandinsky is born; Alfred Nobel invents dynamite in Germany

~1867~

Another Exposition Universelle is held in Paris and after 200 years of Japan not trading with the West, a stand shows Japanese artefacts

~1868~

Louisa M. Alcott writes *Little Women*

~1869~

Matisse is born; in Paris, as sixteen year old Vincent starts his job at the art dealer's Goupil, the future Impressionists are producing their revolutionary art and discussing their ideas

~1870~

The French fight the Germans during the Franco-Prussian War

~1873~
Vincent is transferred to London by Goupil's

~1874~
In April, the first Impressionist exhibition is held in Paris; Vincent is sent to Paris, returning to London after two months

~1875~
Vincent is transferred to the Paris branch of Goupil; the painters Millet and Corot die

~1876~
Dismissed from Goupil's, Vincent returns to England to teach at a boarding school and sketches while there; Alexander Graham Bell invents the telephone

~1877~
In Amsterdam, Vincent studies theology; Courbet dies

~1879~
Vincent works as a preacher in the Borinage district of Belgium, but is soon dismissed for being over-zealous

~1881~
In Paris, the sixth Impressionist exhibition is held; Picasso is born; Vincent quarrels with his father and moves to The Hague

~1882~
Vincent's uncle Cornelis van Gogh commissions him to

produce twelve pen and ink drawings of The Hague; Georges Braque and Edward Hopper are born; Charles Darwin and Dante Gabriel Rossetti die

~1884~
Vincent sends Theo some of his paintings of peasants and accuses Theo of not trying to sell them, Theo tells him he needs to lighten his palette like the Impressionists; the Statue of Liberty is delivered to New York from Paris

~1885~
Vincent leaves The Netherlands for the last time; he moves to Antwerp in Belgium and discovers Japanese prints

~1886~
The artists Diego Rivera and Oskar Kokoschka are born; Vincent takes art classes at the Antwerp École des Beaux-Arts, but soon moves to Paris to live with Theo; the eighth and final Impressionist exhibition is held; Vincent meets the Impressionists and

Gauguin; he starts studying at painter Fernand Cormon's studio, where he meets Toulouse-Lautrec

~1887~
Vincent organizes an exhibition of Japanese prints at the Café Tambourin in Paris; Queen Victoria celebrates her Golden Jubilee; construction of the Eiffel Tower begins

~1888~
Vincent moves to Arles in southern France, but his hopeful start there ends distressingly; Wilhelm II becomes Emperor of Germany

~1889~
The Eiffel Tower marks another Exposition Universelle that celebrates the centenary of the French Revolution; Vincent spends a lot of time in the St. Remy asylum, fifteen miles from Arles

~1890~
An article about Cézanne, Pissarro, Seurat, and Vincent is published in March, while in July, Vincent dies from his own bullet wound

~1892~
The first retrospective exhibition of Vincent's work is held in the Netherlands

WHAT DID HE SAY?

Here are a few of the many things Vincent said about art:

- "Find things beautiful as much as you can, most people find too little beautiful"

- "The duty of the painter is to study nature in depth and to use all his intelligence, to put his feelings into his work so that it becomes comprehensible to others"

- "Even the knowledge of my own fallibility cannot keep me from making mistakes. Only when I fall do I get up again"

- "One must work and dare if one really wants to live"

- "Paintings have a life of their own that derives from the painter's soul"

- "The fishermen know that the sea is dangerous and the storm terrible, but they have never found these dangers sufficient reason for remaining ashore"

- "The way to know life is to love many things"

- "There is no blue without yellow and without orange"

- "What would life be if we had no courage to attempt anything?"

- "The only time I feel alive is when I'm painting"

- "Happiness... it lies in the joy of achievement, in the thrill of creative effort"

- "I dream of painting and then I paint my dream"

- "I often think that the night is more alive and more richly colored than the day"

- "I put my heart and my soul into my work, and have lost my mind in the process"

- "I see drawings and pictures in the poorest of huts and the dirtiest of corners"

- "I wish they would only take me as I am"

A WORK IN CLOSE-UP

This church is close to the inn where Vincent stayed in the last two months of his life. At the time he was working rapidly, applying paint straight from the tube in thick brushstrokes, completing approximately one painting a day. The picture of this 13th century church has been built up with rhythmic patterned marks flowing across the canvas, including comma-shapes, swirled strokes, dots, and dashes—quite unlike anything any other artist was creating at the time.

Influenced by Japanese prints, Vincent painted dark outlines, filling them with lavish colors.

Complementary colors (red-green, orange-blue, yellow-violet) placed next to each other appear extra vibrant.

Vincent described the painting in a letter to his sister Wil: "...the building appears to be violet-hued against a sky of simple deep blue color, pure cobalt, the stained-glass windows appear as ultramarine blotches, the roof is violet, and partly orange.'

He described the green plants and bright flowers in the foreground "with the pink flow of sunshine in it."

The forked path, painted in small dashes and structure of the church appear to shift and move as there are no straight lines.

The foreground is brightly lit, but the church itself is in shadow – as Vincent said: "neither reflects nor emanates any light of its own."

A woman walks up the path, almost lost in the brushwork. Red roofs are bright against the blue-violet sky with their dividing lines of pure white.

The Church at Auvers-sur-Oise, 1890, oil on canvas, 37 x 29in/94 x 75cm, *Musée d'Orsay, Paris, France*

WHERE TO SEE THIS ARTIST'S WORKS IN THE USA

Here are some of the places in the USA where you can see Vincent's work. It's a good idea to check with the museum or gallery before you visit in case the work you wish to see is not on display.

The Art Institute of Chicago,
Chicago, Illinois
(www.artic.edu)

The Detroit Institute of Arts,
Detroit, Michigan
(www.dia.org)

Fine Arts Museum of San Francisco,
San Francisco, California
(www.famsf.org)

The Guggenheim Museum,
New York City, New York
(www.guggenheim.org)

J. Paul Getty Museum,
Los Angeles, California
(www.getty.edu)

The Metropolitan Museum,
New York City, New York
(www.metmuseum.org)

The Museum of Fine Arts,
Houston, Texas
(www.mfah.org)

The Museum of Fine Arts,
Boston, Massachusetts
(www.mfa.org)

The Museum of Modern Art,
New York City, New York
(www.moma.org)

National Gallery of Art,
Washington D.C.
(www.nga.gov)

The Nelson-Atkins Museum of Art,
Missouri, Illinois
(www.nelson-atkins.org)

Norton Simon Museum,
Pasadena, California
(www.nortonsimon.org)

Yale University Art Gallery,
New Haven, Connecticut
(artgallery.yale.edu)
Albright-Knox Art Gallery,

Buffalo, New York
(www.albrightknox.org)

Brooklyn Museum,
New York City, New York
(www.brooklynmuseum.org)

Carnegie Museum of Art,
Pittsburgh, Pennsylvania
(www.cmoa.org)

Cincinnati Art Museum,
Cincinnati, Ohio
(cincinnatiartmuseum.org)

The Cleveland Museum of Art,
Cleveland, Ohio
(www.clevelandart.org)

Hammer Museum,
Los Angeles, California
(hammer.ucla.edu)

Harvard University Art Museums,
Cambridge, Massachusetts
(www.artmuseums.harvard.edu)

Indianapolis Museum of Art,
Indianapolis, Indiana
(www.imamuseum.org)

Memorial Art Gallery of the University of Rochester,
New York
(magart.rochester.edu)

Minneapolis Institute of Arts,
Minneapolis, Minnesota
(www.artsmia.org)

Philadelphia Museum of Art,
Philadelphia, Pennsylvania
(www.philamuseum.org)

Rhode Island School of Design Museum of Art,
Providence, Rhode Island
(www.risdmuseum.or)

Saint Louis Art Museum,
St. Louis, Missouri
(stlouis.art.museum)

The Barnes Foundation,
Philadelphia, Pennsylvania
(www.barnesfoundation.org)

WHERE TO SEE THIS ARTIST'S
WORKS IN THE REST OF THE WORLD

You can see Vincent's works of art in many places around the world, particularly in Europe. It's a good idea to contact the gallery or museum before you visit, to make sure that the work you wish to see is on display.

The Fitzwilliam Museum at the University of Cambridge, Cambridge, England (*www.fitzmuseum. cam.ac.uk*)

The State Hermitage Museum, St Petersburg, Russia (*www.hermitage museum.org*)

Musée d'Orsay, Paris, France (*www.musee-orsay.fr*)

National Galleries of Scotland, Edinburgh, Scotland (*www.nationalgalleries.org*)

National Gallery of Canada, Ottawa, Canada (*www.gallery.ca*)

National Gallery, London, England (*www.nationalgallery.org.uk*)

Neue Pinakothek, Munich, Germany (*www.pinakothek.de*)

Art Gallery of Ontario, Toronto, Canada (*www.ago.net*)

Rijksmuseum, Amsterdam, The Netherlands (*www.rijksmuseum.nl*)

Van Gogh Museum, Amsterdam, The Netherlands (*www.vangoghmuseum.nl*)

Ashmolean Museum, Oxford, England (*www.ashmolean.org*)

Beyeler Foundation Collection, Riehen, Switzerland (*www.beyeler.com*)

Courtauld Institute of Art, London, England (*www.courtauld.ac.uk*)

Finnish National Gallery, Helsinki, Finland (*kokoelmat.fng.fi*)

E. G. Bürhle Collection, Zurich, Switzerland (*www.buehrle.ch*)

Galleria Nazionale d'Arte Moderna e Contemporanea, Rome, Italy (*www.gnam.arti. beniculturali.it*)

Glasgow Museums, Glasgow, Scotland (*www.glasgow museums.com*)

Groninger Museum, Groningen, The Netherlands (*www.groningermuseum.nl*)

Kröller-Müller Museum, Otterlo, Netherlands (*www.kmm.nl*)

Kunstmuseum Basel, Basel, Switzerland (*www.kunstmuseumbasel.ch*)

Museo Nacional de Bellas Artes, Buenos Aires, Argentina (*www.mnba.org.ar*)

National Museum of Wales, Cardiff, Wales (*www.museumwales.ac.uk*)

The New Art Gallery, Walsall, England (*www.thenewartgallery walsall.org.uk*)

New Carlsberg Glyptotek, Copenhagen, Denmark (*www.glyptoteket.dk*)

Palazzo Ruspoli, Rome, Italy (*www.fondazionememmo.com*)

The Pushkin State Museum of Fine Arts, Moscow, Russia (*www.museum.ru*)

Staatsgalerie Stuttgart, Stuttgart, Germany (*www.staatsgalerie.de*)

Tate Modern, London, England (*www.tate.org*)

Thyssen-Bornemisza Museum, Madrid, Spain (*www.museothyssen.org*)

The Whitworth Art Gallery, Manchester, England (*www.whitworth. manchester.ac.uk*)

Von der Heydt-Museum, Wuppertal, Germany (*www.von-der-heydt-museum.de*)

Wallraf-Richartz-Museum, Cologne, Germany (*www.museenkoeln.de*)

FURTHER READING & WEBSITES

BOOKS

Vincent van Gogh
(Great Names),
Richard Bowen,
Mason Crest Publishers,
2002

Vincent Van Gogh:
Portrait of an Artist,
Jan Greenberg,
Corgi Yearling Books, 2003

Van Gogh and Friends
Art Book: With Cezanne,
Seurat, Gauguin, Rousseau
and Toulouse-Lautrec,
Wenda Brewster O'Reilly,
Birdcage Press LLC, 2004

Coloring Book Vincent
van Gogh,
Annette Roeder,
Prestel Coloring Books, 2009

Vincent van Gogh;
The Starry Night,
Richard Thomson,
The Museum of Modern
Art, 2008

Vincent Van Gogh:
Sunflowers and Swirly Stars
(Smart about the Arts),
Joan Holub,
Grosset & Dunlap, 2001

Vincent van Gogh
(The Life and Work of),
Sean Connolly,
Heinemann Library, 2006

Vincent van Gogh
(Great Artists),
Adam G. Klein,
Checkerboard Books, 2006

Art on the Wall:
Post-Impressionism,
Jane Bingham,
Heinemann Library, 2009

Post-Impressionism
(Flying Start),
Pam Cutler,
Barrington Stock Ltd, 2004

Discovering Great Artists,
MaryAnn F. Kohl,
Kim Solga,
Brilliant Publications, 2003

WEBSITES

www.ibiblio.org/wm/paint/auth/van gogh/

www.theartgallery.com.au/kidsart/
learn/van gogh/

www.atelier-van gogh

www.vangoghgallery.com

www.vggallery.com

www.ibiblio.org/wm/paint/auth/gogh/

www.expo-vangogh.com

www.bbc.co.uk/history/historic_figures/
van_gogh_vincent.shtml

www.nga.gov/education/classroom/self_
portraits/act_van_gogh_self.shtm

www.youtube.com/watch
?v=O5tKG39G6Qk

www.vangoghmuseum.nl/vgm/
index.jsp?lang=en

www.nationalgallery.org.uk/
artists/vincent-van-gogh

www.bc.edu/bc_org/avp/cas/fnart/art/
vangogh.htmlcoe.nevada.edu/
mphillips/index.htm

www.ibiblio.org/wm/paint/auth/gogh/self/

www.moma.org/collection/browse_results
.php?object_id=79802

www.kidskonnect.com/subject-index/21-
people/421-van-gogh-vincent.html

www.metmuseum.org/explore/van_gogh
/intro.html

www.kyrene.k12.az.us/schools/brisas/
sunda/art/vangogh.htm

www.mykidsart.com.au/Vincent_van_
Gogh_Famous_Artists_My_Kids_Art.html

www.thekidswindow.co.uk/News/Vincent
_van_Gogh

www.artonstamps.org/vangogh.htm

www.metmuseum.org/toah/hd/gogh/hd_
gogh.htm

GLOSSARY

Abstraction—In art, abstraction refers to ways that some artists distort or eliminate recognizable objects. Abstractions usually show real things being distorted, while abstract art does not show anything recognizable. Both emphasize things other than actual objects, such as emotions

Communard—Communards were members of the Paris Commune that fought against the French army in 1871 following the Franco-Prussian War. The Commune was ruthlessly suppressed, leading to the death of over 20,000

Communards. Vincent's friend and supplier of art materials, "Père" Tanguy, was a former Communard

Composition—Often used as a general term meaning "painting," composition also means the arrangement of elements in a picture

Expressionism—An art movement that began during the early part of the twentieth century in which artists emphasized their personal experiences and feelings

Gauguin—Vincent's friend who developed a style of painting which rejected naturalistic representation

in favor of expressing mood and emotion through bright colors separated by black lines. He called this Synthetism

Icon—Icon originates from the Greek word for image and originally meant a picture of a Saint or Christ. The rules for painting icons remained the same for nearly 1,000 years

Impasto—An Italian word which is used to describe the thickness of paint on the surface of a painting. Impasto is paint that is applied so thickly that it stands proud of the surface and brush marks are clearly evident

Pigment—This usually refers to colored powder that is mixed with a liquid to make paint, such as oil for oil paints

Post-Impressionism—This describes several artists who followed on from Impressionism and generally focused on personal expression, making use of color theories

Salon des Artistes Indépendants—The Salon was originally the only place where artists could exhibit their work in Paris. A jury limited the number of paintings which could be shown

INDEX

47

ACKNOWLEDGMENTS

Picture Credits t=top, b=bottom, c=center, l=left, r=right, OFC=outside front cover.

Art Institute of Chicago. Photo © AKG London; 14tr, 15cr; 32/33cb. The Art Institute of Chicago, IL/Giraudon/The Bridgeman Art Library; OFCt. Christie's Images; 33br. Christie's Images/Bridgeman Art Library, London; 11tr. Courtauld Gallery, London/Bridgeman Art Library, London; 12/13t, 18tl & 28bl. David Sellman; 14/15. Fine Art Photographic Library, London; 22bl, 23tr. Groninger Museum, Groningen. Photo © AKG London; 9cr. © The Guardian (The British Library); 34/35cb. Hahnloser Collection, Bern. Photo © AKG London; & 20/21ct. Mary Evans Picture Library; 6tl, 6br, 7t, 7br, 32l. Metropolitan Museum of Art, New York/ Bridgeman Art Library, London; 14cr. Musee d'Orsay, Paris. Photo © AKG London/Erich Lessing; 27b, 20cl, 31br. Musée d'Orsay, Paris/Giraudon/The Bridgeman Art Library; OFC (main image), OFCb. Musee Rodin, Paris. Photo © AKG London/Erich Lessing; 12c. Musee Toulouse-Lautrec, Albi. Photo © AKG London/Erich Lessing; 10bl. Museum Folkwang, Essen. Photo © AKG London/Erich Lessing; 22cr. Museum of Modern Art, New York. Photo © AKG London; 29t. Museum of Modern Art, New York/The Bridgeman Art Library; OFCc. National Gallery, London/Index/Bridgeman Art Library, London; 35. National Gallery, London. Photo © AKG London/Erich Lessing; 22bl. Photo © AKG London; 8/9cb, 19tr. Photo © Christie's/AKG London; 13cl. Private Collection/Bridgeman Art Library, London; 30tl. Private Collection, New York/Bridgeman Art Library, London; 11br. Pushkin Museum, Moscow/Bridgeman Art Library, London; 33tr. Pushkin Museum, Moscow. Photo © AKG London; 30cr. Rijksmuseum Kroeller-Mueller, Otterlo. Photo © AKG London; 15cl. Rijksmuseum Kroeller-Mueller, Otterlo. Photo © AKG London/Erich Lessing; 21br, 30tr. Rijksmuseum Vincent van Gogh, Amsterdam. Photo © AKG London; 9tl, 13cb, 34tl. Science Museum/Science & Society Picture Library; 7c. © Tate Gallery, London; 10/11cb, 16/17b, 34c. Tate Gallery, London. Photo © AKG London/Erich Lessing; 10/11ct. Van Gogh Museum (Vincent van Gogh Foundation), Amsterdam 8bl, 17tl, 17cl, 18/19bc, 19br, 22/23cb, 25t. Vincent van Gogh, Dutch, 1853-1890, Self-Portrait, oil on artist's board mounted on cradled panel, 1886/87, 41 x 32.5cm, Joseph Winterbotham Collection, 1954.326, photograph © 1996, The Art Institute of Chicago. All Rights Reserved; 15br.

NOTE TO READERS